September 1991

To Bo.

My favorite
climbing partner.

Love; Mom

MOUNTAIN CLIMBING

MOUNTAIN CLIMBING

by Jerolyn Ann Nentl

Library of Congress Catalog Card Number: 80-415

International Standard Book Numbers:
0-89686-075-2 Library Bound
0-89686-079-5 Paperback

Designed and produced by Randal M. Heise

Edited by - Dr. Howard Schroeder
            Prof. in Reading and Language Arts
            Dept. of Elementary Education
            Mankato State University

Library of Congress
Cataloging in Publication Data

Nentl, Jerolyn Ann.
  Mountain climbing.

  (Funseekers)
  SUMMARY: An introduction to the sport of mountain
climbing and to some of the world's famous peaks.
  1. Mountaineering--Juvenile literature. (1. Mountaineer-
ing) I. Schroeder, Howard. II. Title. III. Series
GV200.N46   796.5'22   80-415
ISBN 0-89686-075-2

Photo Credits

David Hiser: 3, 19B, 31
Galen Rowell: Cover, 4, 19A, 20, 21A, 21B, 22, 28, 32
Jonathan T. Wright: 6, 16, 23, 24, 25
Randal M. Heise: 9
American Alpine Club: 11
Bettmann Archive: 12
United Press International: 13, 26, 30

Kirk was high up the side of the mountain on a ridge. It was the final approach to the summit. He climbed carefully with a steady rhythm. Each step had become an effort for him and his partners. Only their desire to stand on the top kept them going.

Kirk loved the mountains. As a teenager, he had hiked in the foothills of the mountains many times. He had been afraid to climb too high then, but now he felt ready to conquer the peaks. He had studied how to safely climb mountains. He had also bought good equipment. Kirk knew his own limits, too. He would tell his climbing partners if the route got too tough for him.

Slowly, he kicked first one foot and then the other into the snow. He breathed deeply and evenly. Every muscle ached. His body was cold and tired. Kirk leaned on his ice axe and took a few more steps. Then there was nothing above him but bright blue sky. At last he was standing on top of the mountain!

Mountains were formed thousands of years ago. People have been climbing them for only a few hundred years. The first to be explored were the Alps, the great mountain chain of Europe: Early travelers feared these high places. They believed that evil spirits lived in the mountains. To them, mountain peaks were the homes of the gods.

By 1700, people were becoming less superstitious. They wanted to know more about nature. One of these men was Hoarce de Saussure of Switzerland. Hoarce loved the mountains. He wanted to learn as much about them as he could. It was the moving rivers of ice, called glaciers, that he wanted to know about most. In 1760, he offered a prize to the first person who climbed Mont Blanc. Mont Blanc is the highest peak in the Alps. It stands 15,782 feet above sea level. No one claimed Hoarce's prize for twenty-six years. At last, in 1786, Jacques Balmat and Dr. Michel Paccard made it to the summit. They climbed up and back in a single day! It took a great deal of courage.

After the Mont Blanc climb, men became more daring. They tried climbing higher. Along the way, they found beautiful meadows and steep rock walls. There were deep gorges and ridges as sharp as knives. Often there were huge cracks in the glaciers. These they called *crevasses*. Sometimes rocks fell down the mountainsides and climbers had to run for their lives. Snow and ice slid down the mountainsides, too. These slides were called *avalanches*.

The Swiss climbers learned the Alps well. They began to work as guides for the wealthy tourists from England. It was they who developed the sport of mountain climbing during the 1800's. Climbing soon spread to the Alps of Austria, Italy, and France. It was called a rich man's sport. Only the rich could afford to hire guides.

Although he was not rich, Edward Whymper was one of the climbing pioneers. He was a struggling young artist from England. He first saw the Matterhorn in 1860. This majestic peak is on the border between Switzerland and Italy. It stands 14,872 feet above sea level. Whymper tried to climb it the next year, but failed. For five years, he tried again and again. Finally he made it to the top in 1865. It was his eighth try. There was much joy at the summit, but it did not last long. On the way down, four of the seven climbers in Whymper's party were killed. People in England were angry. They believed mountain climbing was too dangerous, and felt is should be outlawed.

Edward Whymper (inset photo taken during his early climbing days.)

Such talk did not last long. It could not stop people from climbing. They had felt what it was like to stand on top of a mountain! Instead, the sport became more popular. People began climbing in the United States during the 1800's. By 1883, the Himalayan Mountain Range in Asia had been explored. Women also became interested in climbing. However, the bulky long skirts they wore made climbing very difficult.

There are mountains to climb on every continent. Mt. Everest is the highest peak in the world. It stands on the Nepal-Tibet border in the Himalayas. The mountain is more than 29,000 feet above sea level. No one climbed that high until 1953. In that year Sir Edmund Hillary, of New Zealand, made it to the summit with the help of an oxygen mask. Mount McKinley in Alaska is the tallest peak in North America. It stands 20,270 feet above sea level. Man first climbed to its peak in 1913.

Long dresses didn't stop these early women climbers. This photograph was taken in about 1885.

Sir Edmund Hillary

The main mountain range of South America is the Andes. The range stretches more than four thousand miles along the west coast of that continent. The highest peak in the Andes is called Aconcagua. It stands 22,835 feet above sea level and is the highest peak in either of the Americas. Aconcagua is in Argentina. A mountain called Kilimanjaro is the highest peak in Africa. It stands 19,565 feet above sea level.

Men and women climb mountains because they want to, not because they must. They climb to:
- have fun,
- get away from the crowded cities,
- enjoy the wilderness,
- experience teamwork,
- learn the power of their own bodies,
- better know themselves in the face of danger.

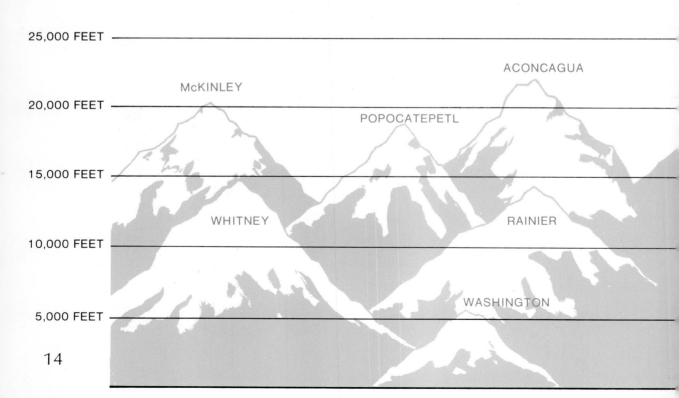

There are many kinds of climbing. Some climbers might spend a day climbing the rocks along the Potomac River. This is called *scrambling*. Others might take a weekend to climb Mt. Rainier in Washington State. Expert climbers may go on expeditions that last for months. There are no trails for these climbers. Sometimes there are not even maps. Expedition climbers often are true explorers. They may go where no one has ever before climbed.

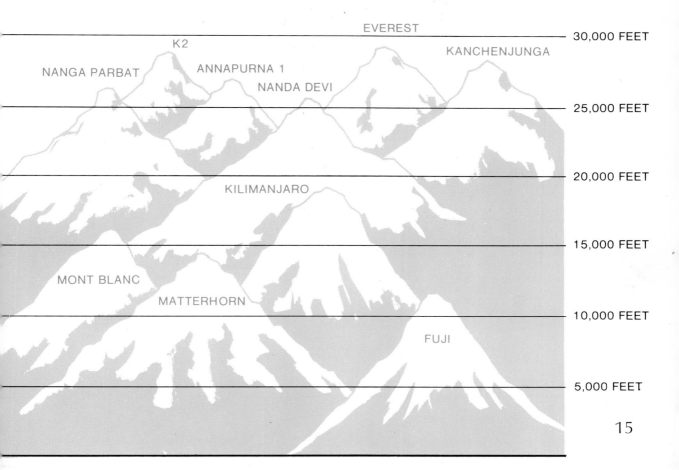

EVEREST

K2   30,000 FEET

KANCHENJUNGA

NANGA PARBAT   ANNAPURNA 1

NANDA DEVI

25,000 FEET

20,000 FEET

KILIMANJARO

15,000 FEET

MONT BLANC

MATTERHORN

10,000 FEET

FUJI

5,000 FEET

15

In 1978, an American team climbed the peak called K2 in the Himalayas. K2 is the second highest mountain in the world. It stands 28,250 feet above sea level. There were fourteen team members, and they used nine tons of equipment to get to the top! The team hired three hundred fifty men, called porters, to help with the gear. They carried it more than one hundred miles from the nearest road to the team's base camp at the foot of the mountain. From the base camp, they carried it in relays to six other camps. Each camp was closer to the peak than the last. From Camp VI, four members of the team made it to the top.

That same year, an all-woman expedition climbed the mountain called Annapurna I. This is another peak in the Himalayas. Annapurna I rises 26,504 feet above sea level. Two of the ten women made it to the summit. Two others died while trying to reach the top.

Most climbers will never go as high as Mt. Everest, K2, or Annapurna I. They will stay closer to home. Many will climb peaks such as Mt. Rainer, outside Seattle, Washington, which stands 14,408 feet above sea level. Mt. Rainer's summit is a two-day's trip for most climbers. During 1978, 6,436 people tried to climb it. About half of them made it to the top. Some went in small groups of two or three. Others went on one of the many large climbs given by the mountain guide service.

People can learn how to climb in many ways. There are special climbing schools and climbing clubs. A beginner might also learn from an experienced climber. There is no easy way to become an expert. There are no short cuts. A beginner must learn how to:

- use a variety of climbing techniques,
- choose the proper equipment,
- map a route up the mountain,
- judge the dangers of the climb, and
- read the weather.

Climbers must learn these lessons well. Their lives may depend on it!

Climbers also need basic camping gear. This gear includes maps, a compass, warm clothing, backpacks, sleeping bags, tents and good boots. There are many kinds of boots. Some are very lightweight and look like shoes. These are flexible and meant only for rock climbing. Others are heavy, with much built-in support for the feet and ankles. These are to be worn when hiking cross-country or on trails and when crossing snow and ice. Mountain climbers will also carry ropes, ice axes, crampons, pitons and carabiners.

Ropes are needed most whether the climb is up the face of a dry rock or a snowy slope. When roped together, climbers become a team. There might be two, three or four climbers to a rope team. When in dangerous areas, the first rule of safety is to *rope up.*

Camp kitchen at 17,300 ft. on Mt. McKinley, Alaska.

You can see why it's so important to "rope up."

Mountain climbers travel in groups, called parties. One climber, called the leader, directs the climb. A group climbs single file. One person at a time does the work. A group might climb straight up a slope or zig-zag from one side of the slope to the other. Sometimes a team must go sideways, straight across a rock face or a mountain slope. This is not a waste of time. It may be the only way the team can continue its climb up or down. It is called a *traverse*.

A dangerous "traverse."

At left, pitons are pounded into the cracks. At right, a rope is put through a carabiner.

When on rocks, the climbers grasp ledges and get handholds or footholds in the cracks. Cracks wide enough for a climber's body are called *chimneys*. Climbers push their feet against one side of the chimney and their hands against the other side to move slowly up or down. When there is nothing to hold onto, climbers must use ropes. To do this they pound metal spikes, or pitons, into small cracks. A snaplink, called a carabiner, hooks onto the piton. The rope is slipped through the carabiner. Sometimes there are no cracks to hold the pitons. In these cases, rock climbers drill holes and insert bolts to hold their ropes. The last climber up the mountain removes the pitons. This is called *"cleaning the pitch."* Bolts remain on the mountain. Climbing up a fixed rope is called *prusikking*.

Rock climbing can be very technical. It is a sport in itself for some people. They enjoy its challenge and never go onto the mountain slopes.

Climbers who climb snowy slopes must learn other techniques. *Stepkicking* is one of them. This means kicking the foot firmly into the snow. It sets the boot securely, and might help keep a climber from slipping. If the snow is too hard, climbers use their ice axes to cut steps. An ice axe also has many other uses. It helps steady a climber. An ice axe can serve as a brake to help stop a climber from sliding down a slope. Digging the ice axe into snow or ice to stop such a slide is called an *arrest*.

Belaying is a safety measure all climbers should know. It means wraping the climbing rope around something that will not move. This might be a large rock or an ice axe that has been jammed into the snow. Then, if a climber slips, other members of the team will be able to hold back on the rope. Done correctly, a belay can save a climber from falling.

"Belaying"

Sure-footed ice climber.

Crampons can help prevent a climber from slipping, too. These are steel frames with sharp points. They fit onto the bottom of a climber's boots. A climber must stamp all the points firmly into the slope with each step.

Goggles protect a climber's eyes. Without them, the glare of the sun can cause snow blindness. Although it goes away, snow blindness can be very painful. Goggles protect a climber's eyes from high winds and blowing bits of ice, too.

Climbing down a rock or a mountain is much more difficult than going up. For this reason climbers do not always return using the same technique or by the same route. A quick way to descend a short distance is to slide down a rope. This is called a *rappel*. Sliding down

This climber takes a quick trip down using a "rappel."

a snowfield is called a *glissade*. Climbers can glissade standing up or sitting down. They can also use their boots as skis. There are many dangers in each type of descent. Climbers must make sure they can stay in control at all times.

Mountain climbing is a walking sport. Climbers must learn how to walk and breathe correctly. They must also learn how to keep a steady pace. If they do, they can walk long distances without tiring. They will also be able to carry heavy packs of supplies without injury. The first thing climbers must learn is to walk with their weight directly over their feet. This keeps their bodies well balanced. They may crouch just a little. Their hips, knees, and ankles may be slightly bent. They let their leg muscles do all the work. Too often beginners lean into the slope. This only throws them off balance. It may also cause a slip or a bad fall. A climber's breathing must be deep and even, in rhythm with the steps. Pace depends on the length of each climber's legs. It may also vary with the slope of the land. The amount of time allowed for the climb and the weight of the backpack may affect a climber's pace, too.

Well trained climbers can keep up a good pace all day without tiring.

Expert climbers make it look easy, but it is not. It is a difficult and dangerous sport. There were one hundred eighteen climbing accidents in this country reported to The American Alpine Club in 1978. There were forty-two deaths. Eighty-five people were hurt. Ten more people died in Canada. No one knows exactly the number of climbing accidents that take place each year. Many are not reported.

There will always be danger to face in the mountains. There are glaciers and crevasses to be crossed. A climbing partner might get sick from the high altitude. The weather may turn bad at any moment. Sudden avalanches are constant threat in springtime.

Smart climbers follow these basic rules:

- Be in good physical condition. Long-distance running is good exercise.
- Have the right gear and know how to use it. Keep it in good shape at all times.
- Know the different climbing techniques and when to use them. Do not climb beyond your skills.
- Check the overall view of a rock or mountain with care — before starting to climb. Sometimes it is easier to map out a safe route to the top from a distance.
- Always allow plenty of time to reach the top and return before dark. Sometimes a climber might be forced to stay overnight on a mountain without a sleeping bag or tent. This is called a *bivouac*.
- Watch for changing weather conditions.
- Use caution at all times. Watch where you are going with each step. "Rope up" in dangerous areas and probe ahead with your ice axe.
- Never climb alone.
- Always tell someone where you are climbing and when you plan to return.
- Climb only with a good leader, and learn to be one yourself. Good leaders are not daredevils. They are mature people who use common sense and good judgement.

Oxgen masks are needed at very high altitudes.

Modern climbers no longer look for evil spirits in high places. They look for real danger and excitement on the rocks, snow, and ice. The highest mountain in the world has been climbed, but the challenge of the unknown remains. There are many smaller peaks still to be climbed. Some may prove to be more challenging than the higher peaks. Finding new routes to climb old peaks and changing weather conditions also offer a real challenge.

The challenge of the mountains will always be there. Few people, however, risk the dangers to stand on top of them.

After reaching their goal these climbers have their picture taken on the summit.